MW00778325

Disaster
Super Heroes

The Red Cross

by Phoebe Marsh

MODERN CURRICULUM PRESS

Pearson Learning Group

Introduction

A woman and two children walk to the spot where their small house once stood. There is nothing left but mud and rocks.

Their beds are gone. Their clothes are gone. The car is gone. Everything they have is gone. They have no money. Even if they did, the whole place has been hard hit by the flood. There is nothing to eat or drink for miles. How will they get food and water in order to survive?

The situation is bad.

But there is help.

When disaster strikes, the Red Cross is a lifeline for thousands of people.

The Red Cross is a volunteer organization that helps people get through emergencies. It also helps them prepare for emergencies before they happen. When people are in trouble—whether it be a few people or a few thousand—the heroes of the Red Cross go to work.

How It All Started

The Red Cross did not begin with a natural disaster, but a catastrophe created by people. A Swiss businessman, Henri Dunant, was traveling in northern Italy at the end of the Battle of Solferino in 1859. He was shocked to find forty thousand dead and seriously injured soldiers scattered about the battlefield.

Dunant begged local townspeople to help the wounded soldiers, regardless of their nationality.

Even after he returned home to Switzerland, Dunant could not forget what he had seen. He wrote a pamphlet, which he distributed to governments throughout Europe. In this pamphlet he asked if it would be possible for all countries to organize permanent groups of volunteers to help the wounded in wartime.

Government officials from twelve countries responded to Dunant's plea. This group drafted a plan in 1864, called the First Treaty of Geneva, to provide help to wounded and sick soldiers in times of war. Now all countries recognized the International Red Cross.

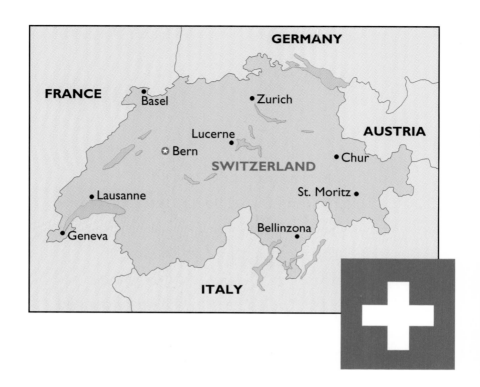

The symbol of the red cross on a white flag was adopted to honor Switzerland, where the Red Cross was born. Switzerland's flag shows a white cross on a red background.

Today the Red Cross helps people all over the world. There are over 175 Red Cross societies and they are in nearly every independent nation on Earth.

Clara Barton's Success

The American Red Cross was founded in 1881 by Clara Barton. This woman was no stranger to the horrors of war. Barton had nursed and fed soldiers during the Civil War, and she had traveled to Europe to help soldiers who were fighting there.

But Barton decided to expand the role of the Red Cross in America by adding disaster relief to the organization's goals. She felt the Red Cross should help out in times of peace as well as in war.

Today the American Red Cross is one of the largest humanitarian organizations in the nation.

From the start, the American Red Cross has relied on volunteers and donations from well-wishers to keep going.

Over one million people are volunteers with the American Red Cross. In fact, close to one-third of all volunteers are eighteen years old or younger!

The Red Cross carefully provides special training for all of its volunteers, no matter what kind of work they are doing.

In addition to these volunteers, many people with special skills (such as doctors and nurses) volunteer their time with the Red Cross.

Who Gives Help? Who Gets Help?

The American Red Cross helps people with all sorts of problems.

The Armed Forces Emergency Services provides help to the men and women in the U.S. Armed Forces. This service helps members of the armed forces and their families to communicate in times of emergency. They assist veterans of war and lead them to other services that can help them meet their needs.

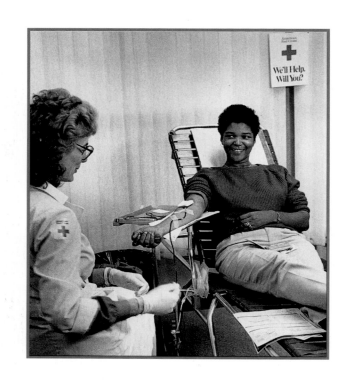

The Biomedical Services is America's biggest supplier of blood and organs for transplants. The Red Cross supplies nearly half of the nation's blood by working with blood donors and hospitals from around the country. So many people are Red Cross blood donors that chances are, someone you know has donated blood during a Red Cross blood drive!

The Health and Safety Services of the Red Cross helps to save lives every day. This service offers many programs in first-aid and CPR (a method used to revive people who have stopped breathing). It also helps people learn how to avoid injuries and save lives in emergency situations. In addition, it offers classes in swimming and water safety!

The largest and most well-known part of the American Red Cross is the Disaster Services division. This arm of the Red Cross provides a number of emergency relief services after a disaster such as a hurricane or a flood. It also offers help in teaching people how to prepare for a disaster and stay safe if one occurs.

No one can predict when a hurricane, a flood, or an earthquake will occur. But when a disaster strikes, the Red Cross is one of the first organizations on the spot. Volunteers work with the victims, local fire fighters, police, and ambulance workers. And they are trained to give whatever help is needed most.

The first step might be getting people to safety.
Before a flood or hurricane hits, the Red Cross tries
to move people to safer areas. When a disaster has
already struck, volunteers help shelter, feed, care for, and
reunite families.

After a disaster, crops are usually destroyed, and stores that sell food are often damaged. Even worse, drinking water is usually polluted. The Red Cross helps by bringing food and water and by providing ways for victims to get new clothing.

The Red Cross opens shelters too, so that people who have lost their homes have a safe place to stay. The shelters may be in houses of worship, schools, or other community buildings. Beds are set up, food is served and first aid is given, if needed.

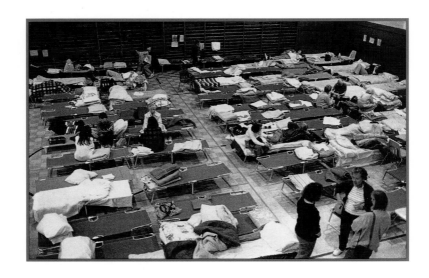

After people are rescued and brought to shelters, the Red Cross helps them get back on their feet. It helps them buy food and clothes. It finds homes for them to rent until they can rebuild.

The Red Cross even provides cleaning kits. Houses and apartments that were flooded or blown apart are often full of mud, dirty water, or broken dishes and glass. Volunteers help clean up even the mightiest of messes.

After the crisis is over, the Red Cross volunteers check homes for damage. If homes can be saved, the Red Cross refers people to agencies that can complete the repairs.

Afterword

It takes time, work, and money to keep the Red Cross super heroes in action. Some of the volunteers are always working, even between disasters, to keep everyone ready for the next one.

Nature is full of surprises. People can't always predict the weather, the mood of a volcano, or the shifting of the Earth's surface. But people can always depend on the Red Cross.